TOBY and his hospital friends

THE PET THERAPY DOG

CHARMAINE HAMMOND

Illustrations by Rose Anne Prevec

Based on the true story, *On Toby's Terms* by Charmaine Hammond. Toby is a pet therapy dog and winner of the CHIMO Reese Award.

If you are unable to order this book from your local bookseller or online, you may order directly from the publisher.

Kendahl House Press is an imprint of Bettie Youngs Book Publishers:
www.BettieYoungsBooks.com

Distributed by SCB Distributors
15608 South New Century Drive
Gardena, CA 90248
800-729-6423
www.SCBdistributors.com

Library of Congress Control Number: 2011907230
ISBN: 978-0-9836045-0-1

Printed in the U.S.A.

"Toby?" calls Miss Charmaine. "Toby, where are you? It's Wednesday!"

Wednesday is Toby's favorite day of the week. Whenever he hears Miss Charmaine call: "Toby, it's Wednesday! Come and get your vest on. It's time to go to the hospital," Toby comes running!

"Oh, I see you brought your favorite stuffed animal to bring to your friends at the hospital. How thoughtful of you, Toby!"

Toby is a pet therapy dog. A therapy dog gets special training so it can go visit people in the hospital and cheer them up.

Toby likes to take his favorite toy, a teddy bear, to show his friends at the hospital.

Toby's vest lets everyone know he has a very special job to do. Toby also has a red bandana that he loves to wear on the days he goes to visit his friends.

This is how Toby looks on Wednesday when he goes to the hospital. Have you ever seen a pet therapy dog?

Toby gets very excited when he knows it is time to see his hospital friends. "You sure are excited, Toby. Okay, then, let's go see who needs cheering up today," says Miss Charmaine.

Does Toby look excited to you?

Miss Charmaine and Toby drive to the hospital. “Toby, today you will see Nurse Nancy, Mrs. Smith, Simon, and all the other children,” Miss Charmaine tells Toby.

"Woof!" says Toby. He is very excited about seeing his hospital friends.

Soon they arrive at the hospital.

"Woof! Woof!" barks Toby. He wants everyone to know that he has arrived.

Everyone is waiting for Toby. "Toby is here! Toby is here!" shout his hospital friends.

Toby sees Nurse Nancy first.

Nurse Nancy gives Toby a big hug. "Hi Toby. Hi Miss Charmaine. We are all so happy to see you."

"Woof! Woof!" barks Toby.

"Shhhhh," says Miss Charmaine. "Not so loud, Toby. You must use your inside voice now."

"Woof," says Toby, this time more quietly.

“Toby, I missed you!” says Simon.
“I am so happy you are here!”

"Toby, I want you to meet Sarah, my new friend. She doesn't feel good and has to have an operation so she can get better. Maybe you can cheer her up."

Suddenly, Toby barks loudly, and it frightens little Sarah. Nurse Nancy sees that Sarah is wearing brown slippers that look just like Toby's little brown teddy bear toy.

Don't be afraid, Sarah," Nurse Nancy tells her. "Toby's favorite toy is a teddy bear that looks very much like your slippers. He thinks you are wearing his teddy bear."

All the children laugh. "Toby, you are silly. Those are slippers on her feet, not toy teddy bears! Sarah is not wearing your favorite toy on her feet!"

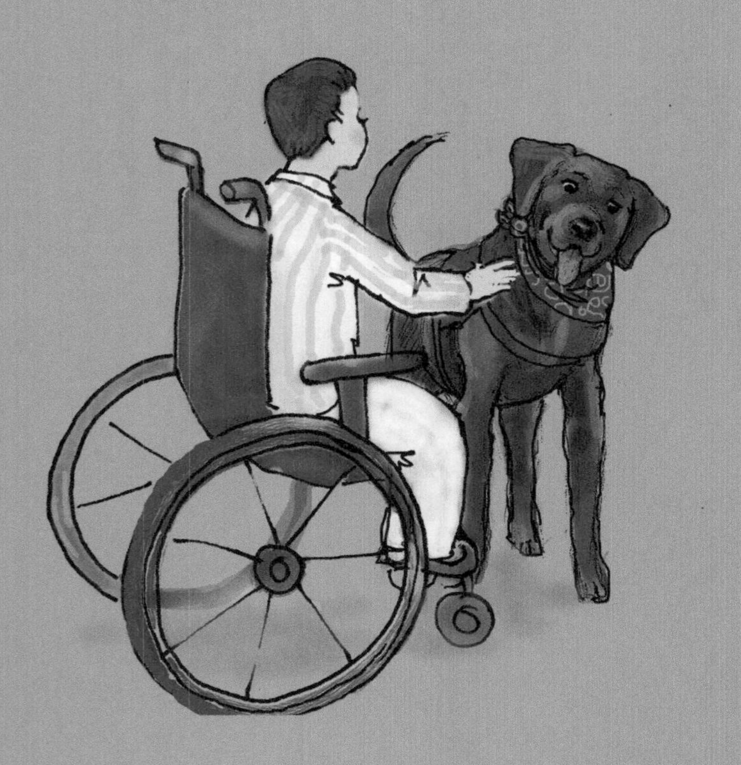

“Toby is barking at your slippers, not you, Sarah,” Simon tells Sarah. “Toby is very gentle. We’re best friends.”

“You are?” Sarah asks.

“We sure are. Toby is the best friend ever. When he first saw me, he put his paw on my lap to show me he wanted to be friends.”

Sarah slowly stretches her furry slipper out to Toby. “These are not your teddy bear toys, Toby,” she tells the big brown dog. Toby wags his tail.

"Every time I hear children laughing out here, I know it must be Wednesday and that Toby is here," says Mrs. Smith, coming into the room where the children have gathered.

"I just love it when Toby helps me go for my walk in the garden. Are you ready to go for our walk, Toby?"

In the garden, Mrs. Smith stops to look at the pretty flowers. When she sits down on the park bench to rest, Toby sits with her and rests his head on her lap. "I once had a dog that looked very much like you, Toby," Mrs. Smith tells Toby.

Mrs. Smith and Toby enjoy their visit together.

“Okay, Toby,” says Mrs. Smith. “That’s all the walking I need for today. Besides, it’s almost story time for the children, so we better go back inside.”

"Where's Miguel?" asks Nurse Nancy. "Let's tell Miguel it is story time."

"Miguel went to his room," says Simon. "I'll go get him, Nurse Nancy. Come on Toby, let's tell Miguel it is story time!"

“A dog, here in the hospital?” asks Miguel. “I wish I could see *my* doggie. I haven’t seen him for three long days. What’s your name, doggie?” Miguel asks Toby.

"His name is Toby," says Miss Charmaine. "Toby thinks you look sad Miguel. Why are you sad?"

"I miss my mom and dad," says Miguel. "And I miss my doggie, too."

Toby runs to get his favorite teddy bear for Miguel.

“That is very kind of you, Toby,” says Miss Charmaine. “Miguel, Toby wants you to hold his favorite toy during story time. Would you like that?”

"I sure would," says Miguel. "Thank you Toby!" Toby lets out a quiet bark, being careful to use his inside voice.

“It’s story time,” says Nurse Nancy. She reads the story to the children, and shows them the pictures in the book.

“I love story time,” shouts Maria. “My mom always reads me stories!”

"Sssshhh," says Simon. "You must use your inside voice. Look, Toby has fallen asleep."

“Okay,” says Nurse Nancy, “story time is over and it’s time for Toby to go. Toby will be back again next Wednesday. Who would like that?”

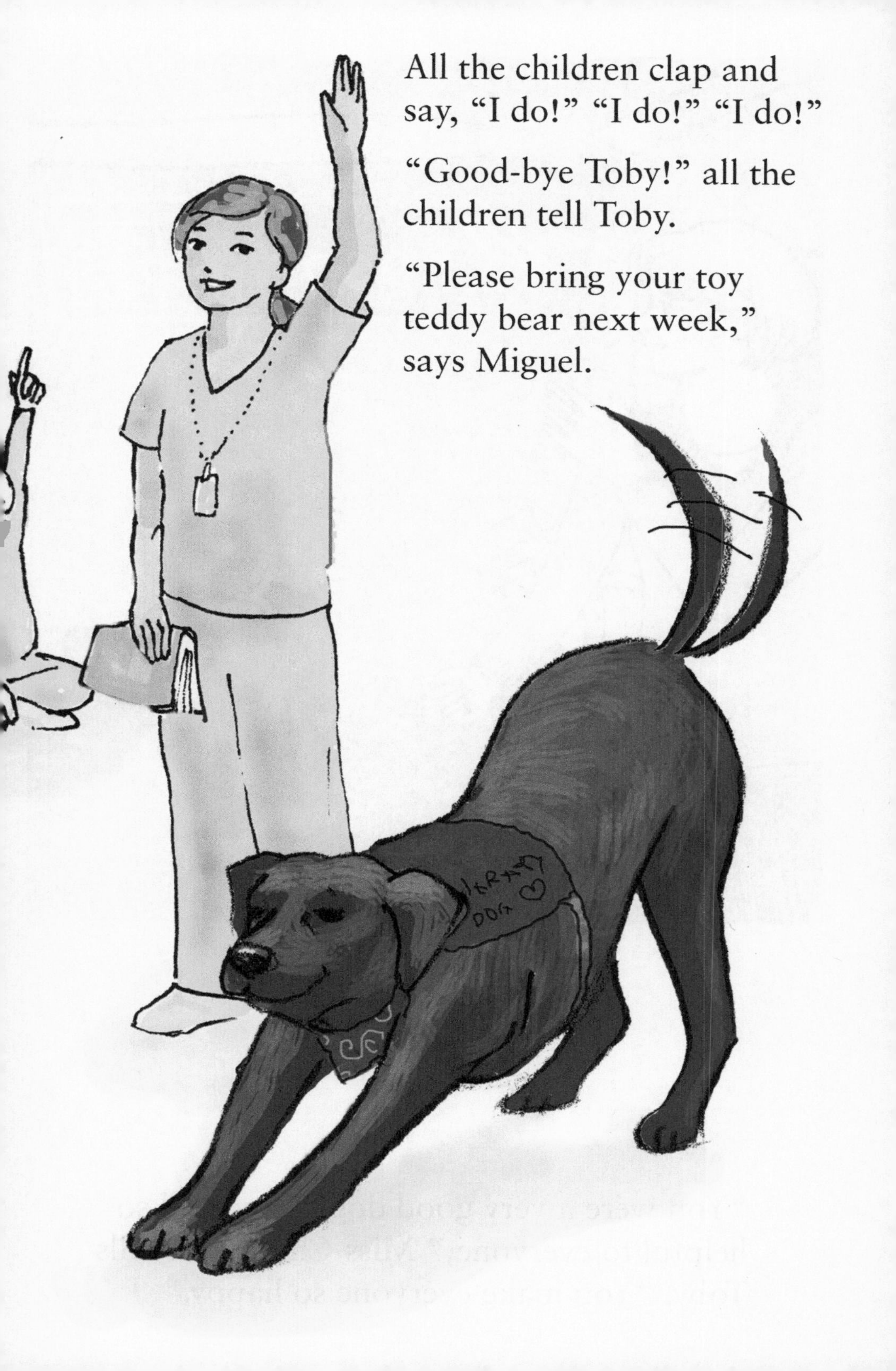

All the children clap and say, “I do!” “I do!” “I do!”

“Good-bye Toby!” all the children tell Toby.

“Please bring your toy teddy bear next week,” says Miguel.

"You were a very good dog, Toby, and so helpful to everyone," Miss Charmaine tells Toby. "You make everyone so happy."

"Woof! Woof! Woof!" Toby barks to his friends.

"See you all next Wednesday," says Miss Charmaine.

Questions to Enhance Children's Critical Thinking Skills

What is Toby's favorite day of the week?

Why was Toby excited to go to the hospital?

What does Toby wear to the hospital when he visits his friends?

Why did Toby bark at Sarah's slippers?

Why was Miguel sad?

Why were the children in the hospital?

Why did the children look forward to Toby coming to the hospital?

Simon said Toby is a very good friend. How was Toby a good friend?

Who are your friends? Why is it important to be a good friend?

Have you done nice things for your friends? What have your friends done for you?

Sarah was afraid of Toby. Have you ever been afraid of a dog? Why?

How does Toby help his friends?

How does Toby make people happy?

What makes you feel really happy?

Toby Fun!

Find Toby in the maze.

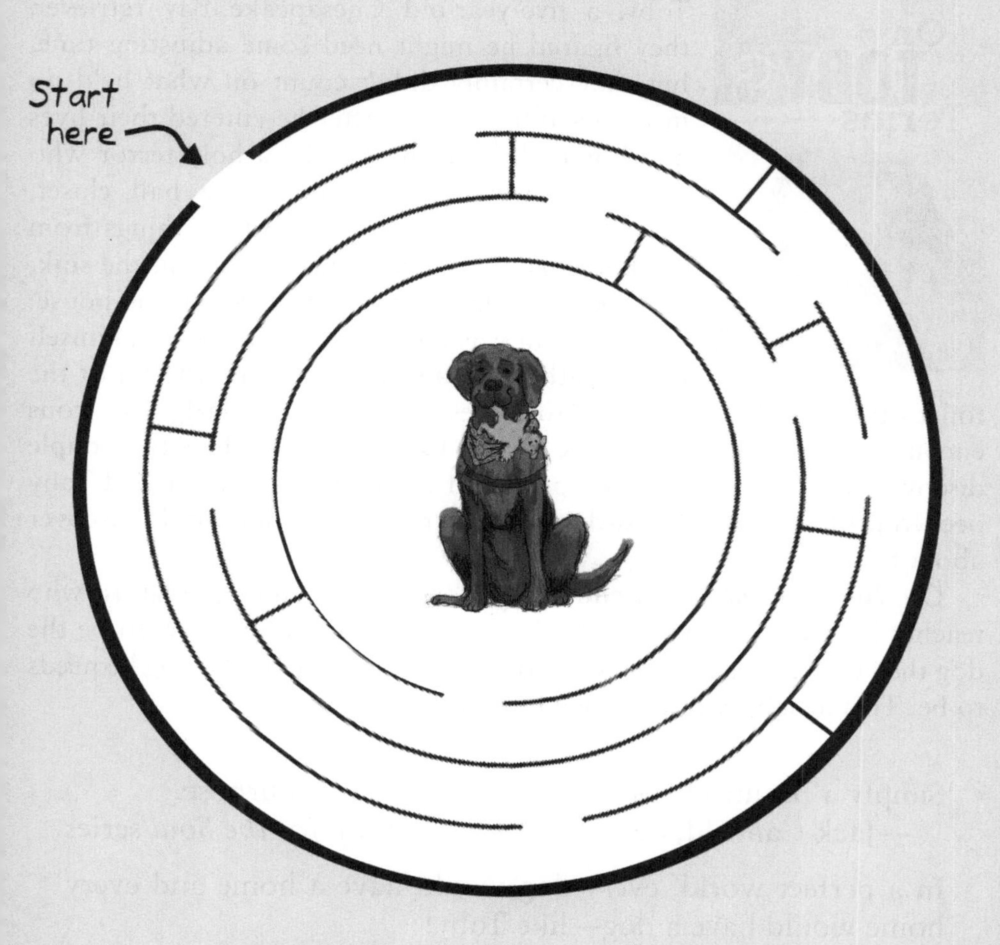

Write your name here.

____

Unscramble the letters to spell a word.

___ ___ ___ ___

B T Y O

CHARMAINE HAMMOND IS ALSO THE AUTHOR OF

ON TOBY'S TERMS

When Charmaine and her husband adopted Toby, a five-year-old Chesapeake Bay retriever, they figured he might need some adjusting time, but they certainly didn't count on what he'd do in the meantime. Soon after he entered their lives and home, Toby proved to be a holy terror who routinely opened and emptied the hall closet, turned on water taps, pulled and ate things from the bookshelves, sat for hours on end in the sink, and spent his days rampaging through the house. Oddest of all was his penchant for locking himself in the bathroom, and then pushing the lid of the toilet off the tank, smashing it to pieces. After a particularly disastrous encounter with the knife-block in the kitchen—and when the couple discovered Toby's bloody paw prints on the phone—they decided Toby needed professional help. Little did they know what they would discover about this dog.

On Toby's Terms is an endearing story of a beguiling creature who teaches his owners that, despite their trying to teach him how to be the dog they want, he is the one to lay out the terms of being the dog he needs to be. This insight would change their lives forever.

Simply a beautiful book about life, love, and purpose.
—Jack Canfield, coauthor *Chicken Soup for the Soul* series

In a perfect world, every dog would have a home and every home would have a dog—like Toby!
—Nina Siemaszko, actress, *The West Wing*

This is a captivating, heartwarming story and we are very excited about bringing it to film.
—Steve Hudis, Producer, IMPACT Motion Pictures

ISBN: 978-0-9843081-4-9 · $14.95

In bookstores everywhere or online, or direct from the publisher,
www.BettieYoungsBooks.com

CPSIA information can be obtained at www.ICGtesting.com
Printed in the USA
LVOW01s0242161013

357063LV00002B/5/P

9 780983 604501